This Book Belongs To

....

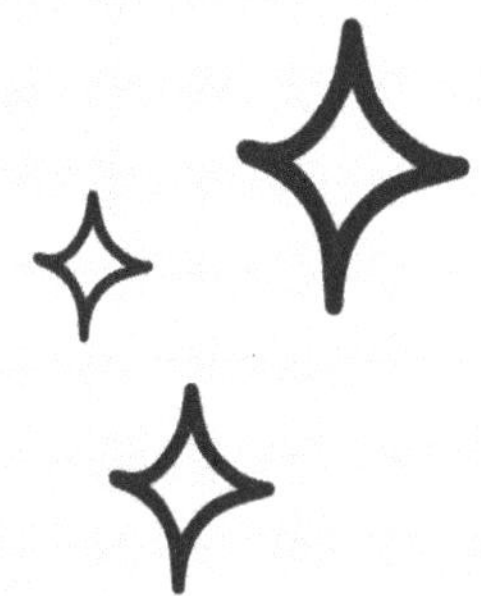

Content

Content

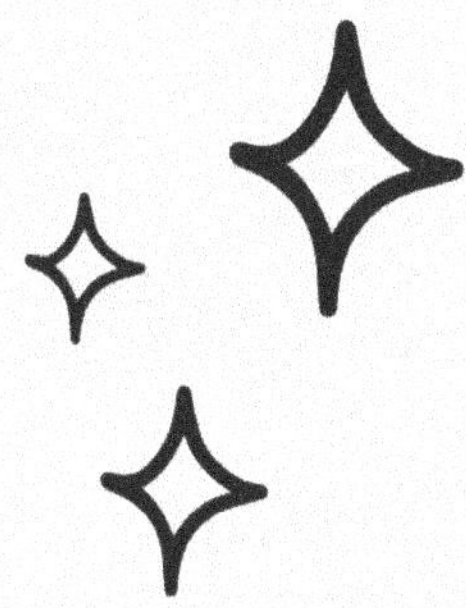

Bella Bunny's
Brave Leap
1

Bella Bunny is nervous about jumping over a stream in the forest.

2

3

One day, a little fox gets stuck
on the other side of the stream.

4

Bella realizes she must overcome her fear to help her friend.

With a deep breath, she takes a leap and makes it across!

Bella learns that courage isn't about not being scared; it's about facing your fears.

Life Lesson: Overcoming Fear
8

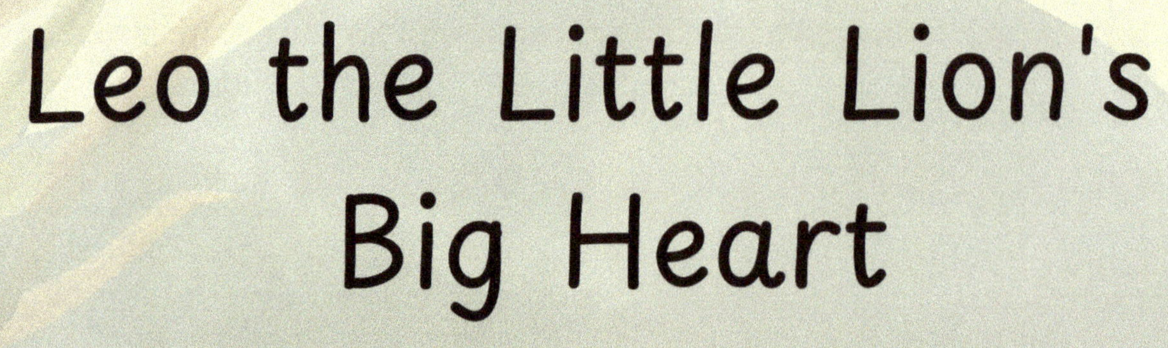

Leo the Little Lion's Big Heart

Leo the Lion feels he must be fierce and strong, just like his father.

However, he often sees his friends upset
and never knows how to help.

One day, he sees a baby elephant
who has lost her way.

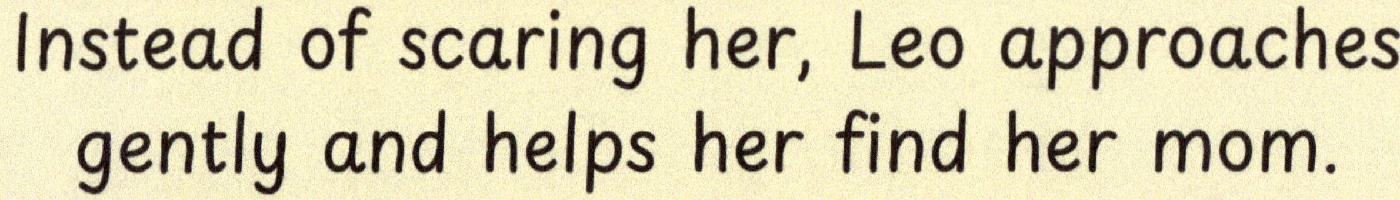

Instead of scaring her, Leo approaches gently and helps her find her mom.

His kindness not only helps the baby elephant but also teaches Leo that being strong is about having a big heart.

Leo new that his dad would be
very proud of him.

Life Lesson: The Power of Kindness

17

18

Excited, she tries to find the treasure on her own but quickly realizes it's too hard.

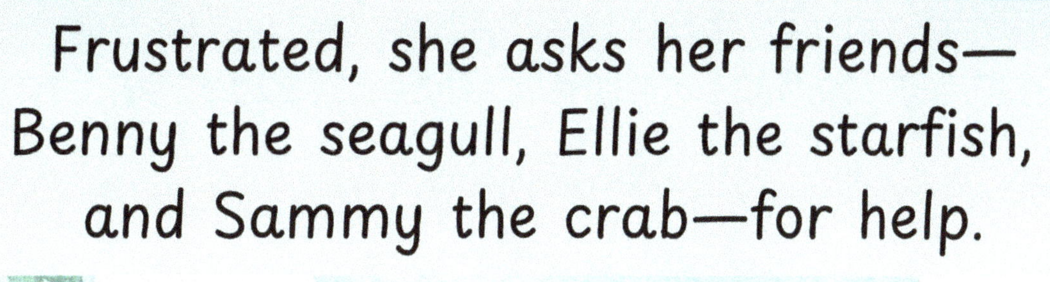

Frustrated, she asks her friends—
Benny the seagull, Ellie the starfish,
and Sammy the crab—for help.

Together, they solve clues and overcome obstacles.

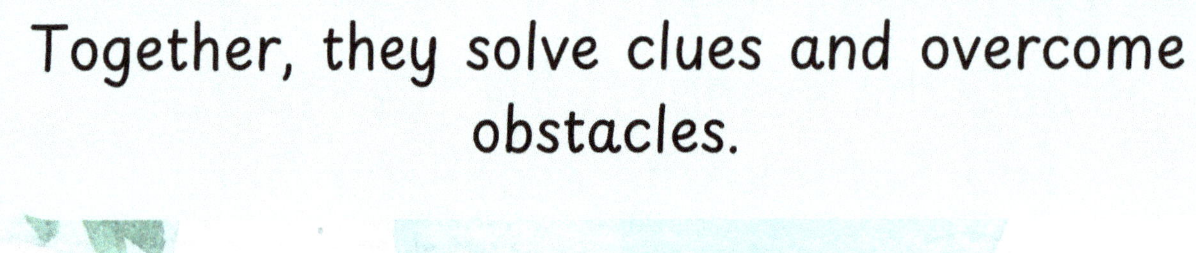

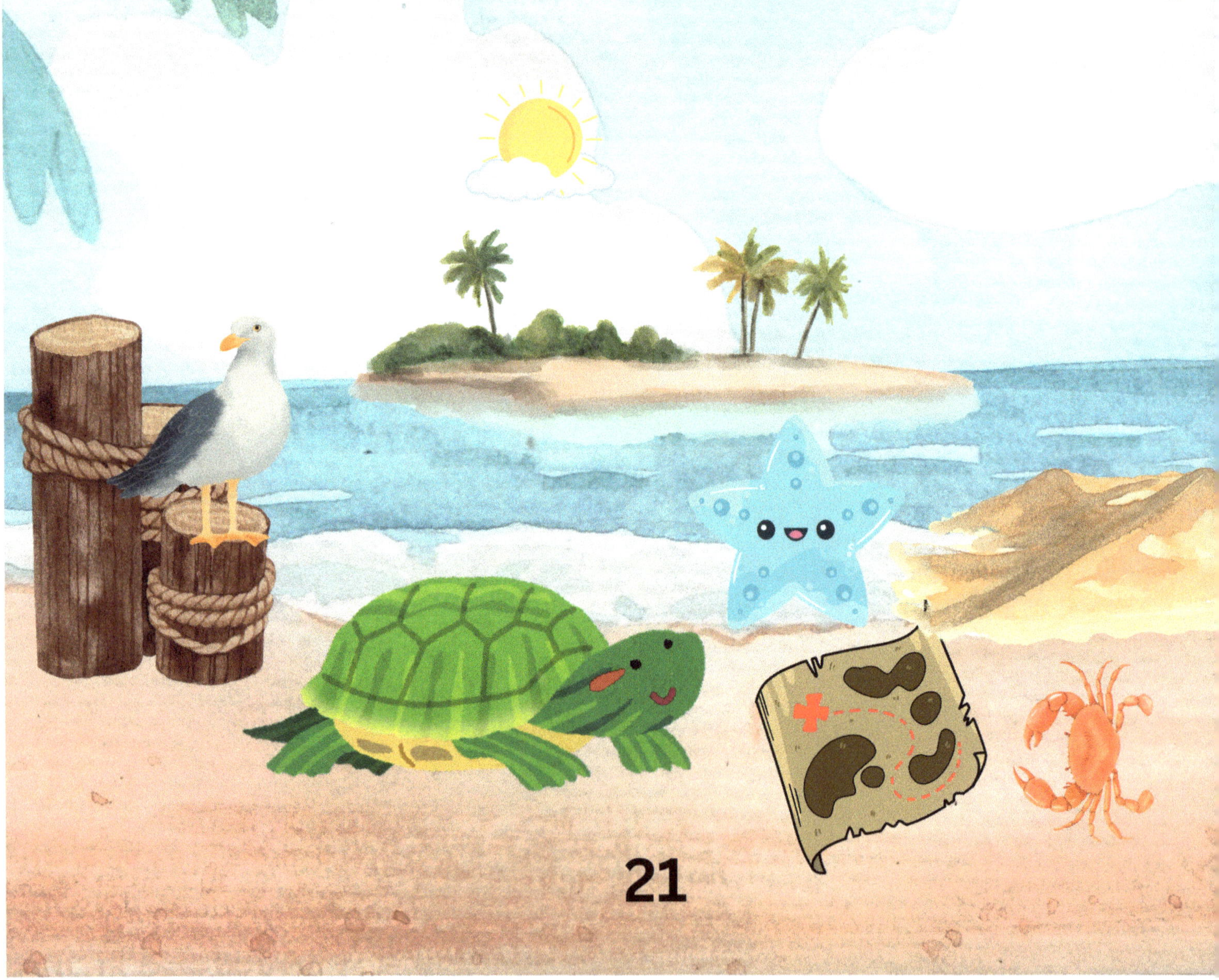

Tilly learns that teamwork makes tasks easier and more fun, and they all share the treasure together.

Tilly learned very impotant lesson today!
23

Life Lesson: The Value of Teamwork
24

Max the Mischievous Monkey
25

Max the Monkey loves playing pranks on his friends. One day, he pretends to see a giant snake, causing a panic.

When everyone realizes it was a joke,
they are not happy with Max.

Feeling guilty, he decides to apologize
and admits the truth.

His friends appreciate his honesty, and they talk about how pranks can hurt feelings

Max learns that honesty builds trust,
and it's always better to tell the truth.

Max was very happy that his friends can trust him again.

Life Lesson: The Importance of Honesty
32

Clara Cat's
Cozy Community

Clara Cat notices that her neighborhood has become quiet, with everyone keeping to themselves.

She decides to host a community picnic to bring everyone together.

At the picnic, they share stories and laughter, reconnecting with one another.

Clara realizes that a strong community is built on friendships and support.
37

They all agree to meet monthly, creating a joyful neighborhood where everyone feels included.

Clara was happy that her picnic turned out to be very positive experience for everyone.
39

Life Lesson: The Strength of Community

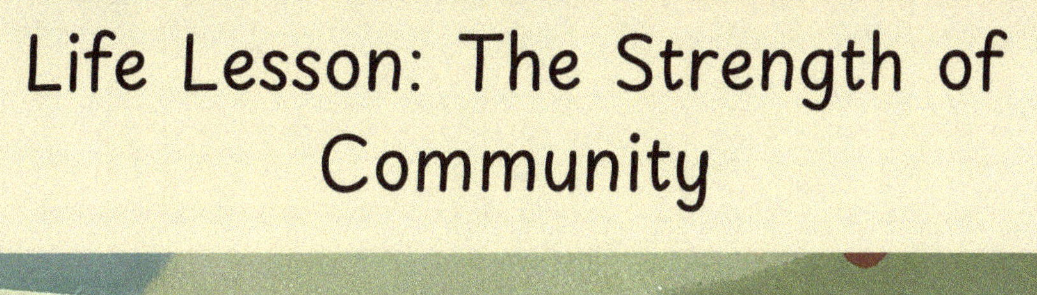

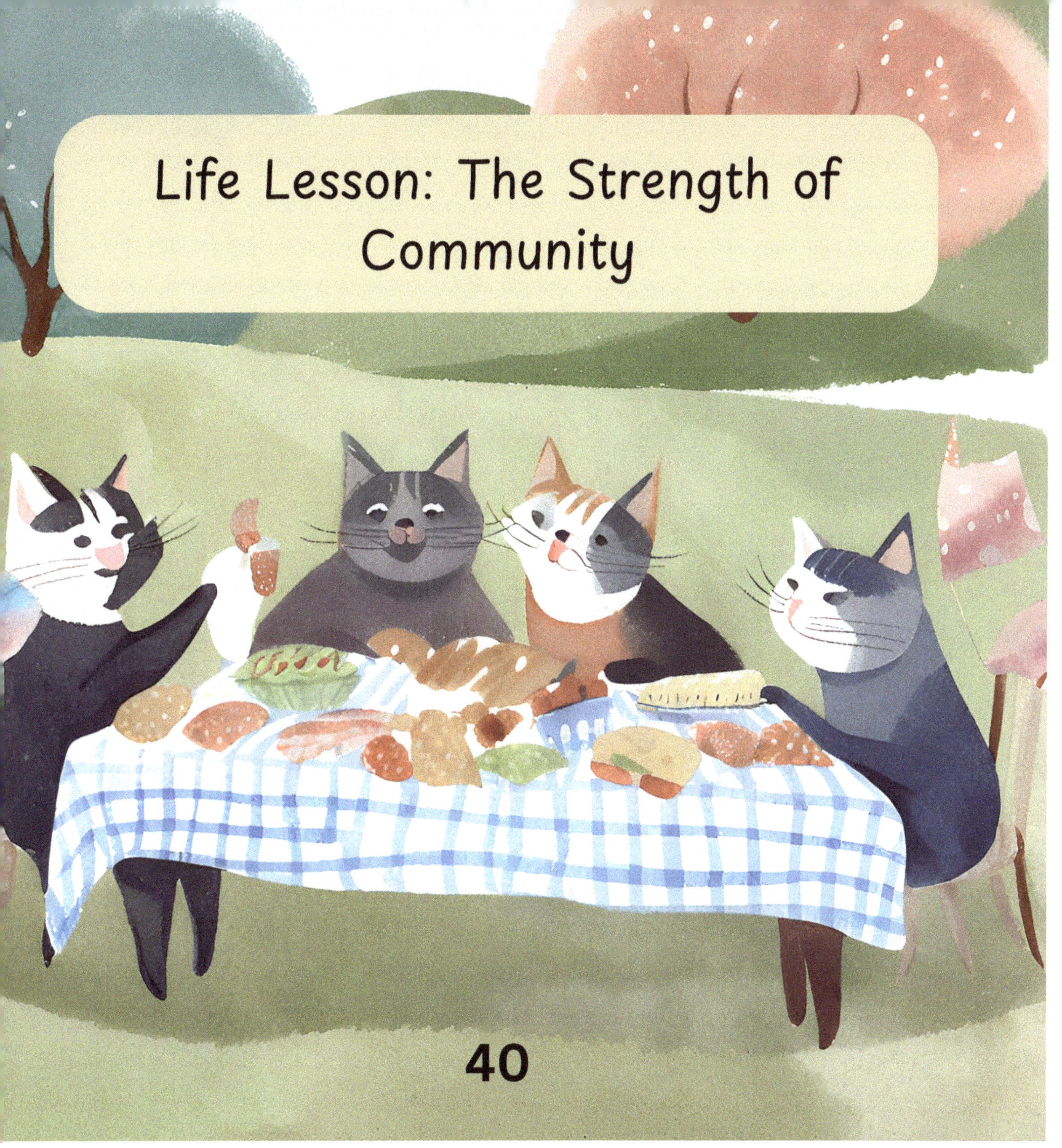

Oliver the Owl's
Wise Words

Oliver the Owl is known as the wisest creature in the forest, but he often talks more than he listens.

42

One day, his friends gather
to share their problems.
43

Instead of jumping in with advice, Oliver decides to listen carefully to each friend.
44

He learns that sometimes the best way to help is to truly understand what someone is feeling.

By the end of the day, Oliver realizes that listening is a powerful tool for friendship.

Oliver was happy that he helped his friends today.

Life Lesson: The Importance of
Listening

Fiona Fox and the Missing Treats

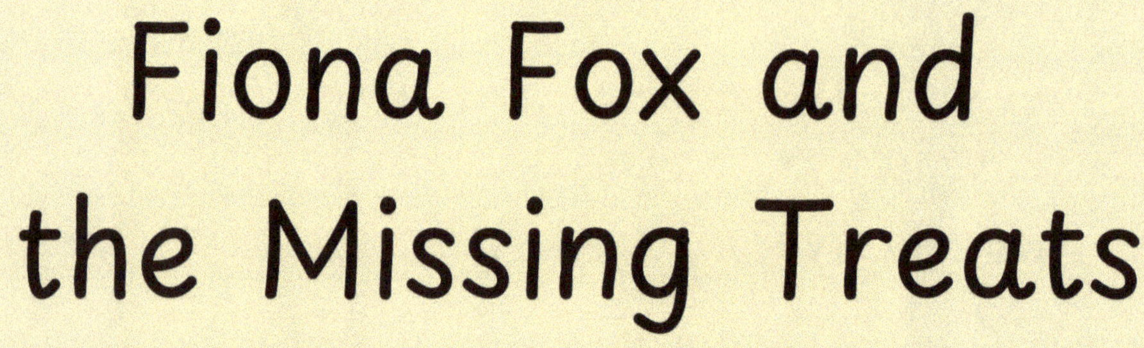

Fiona Fox is known for her cleverness, but she gets caught up in a game of stealing treats from the other animals.

She feels clever at first, but soon, her friends find out and feel hurt.

Fiona realizes that cheating doesn't just affect others; it can ruin friendships too.

To make things right, she apologizes and returns the treats, promising to play fair from now on.

53

Fiona learns that honesty is the best policy and that being fair brings everyone joy.

Fiona decided that from now on she will be honest with her friends.

Life Lesson: The Consequences
of Cheating

Benny the Bear's
Big Idea
57

58

His friends are skeptical and think it's too hard.
59

Instead of giving up, Benny uses his
creativity to brainstorm ideas.
60

He gathers supplies and asks his friends for help.

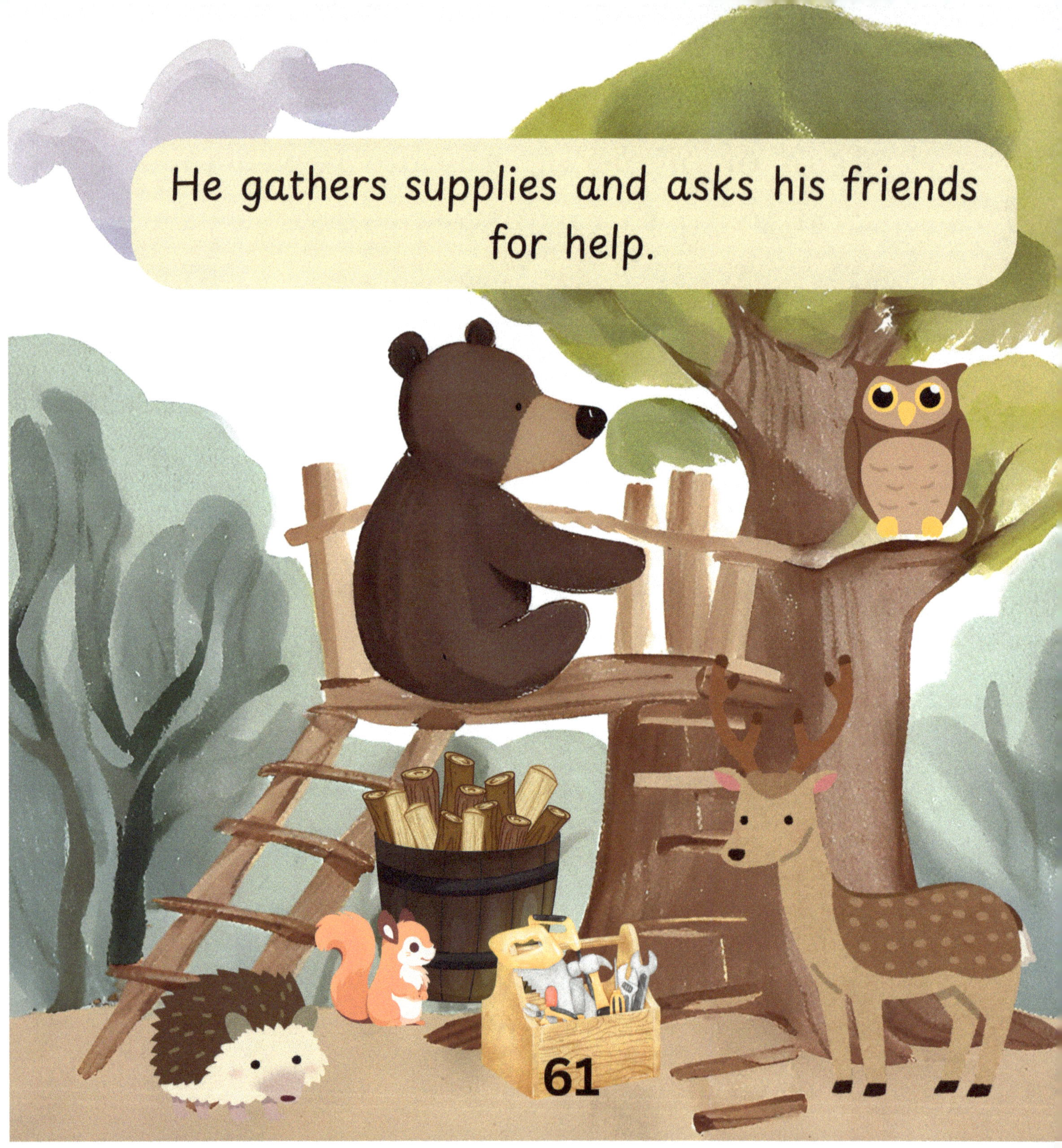

Together, they come up with fun designs and build a fantastic treehouse!

Benny learns that embracing creativity can turn dreams into reality, especially when you work together.

Life Lesson: Embracing
Creativity

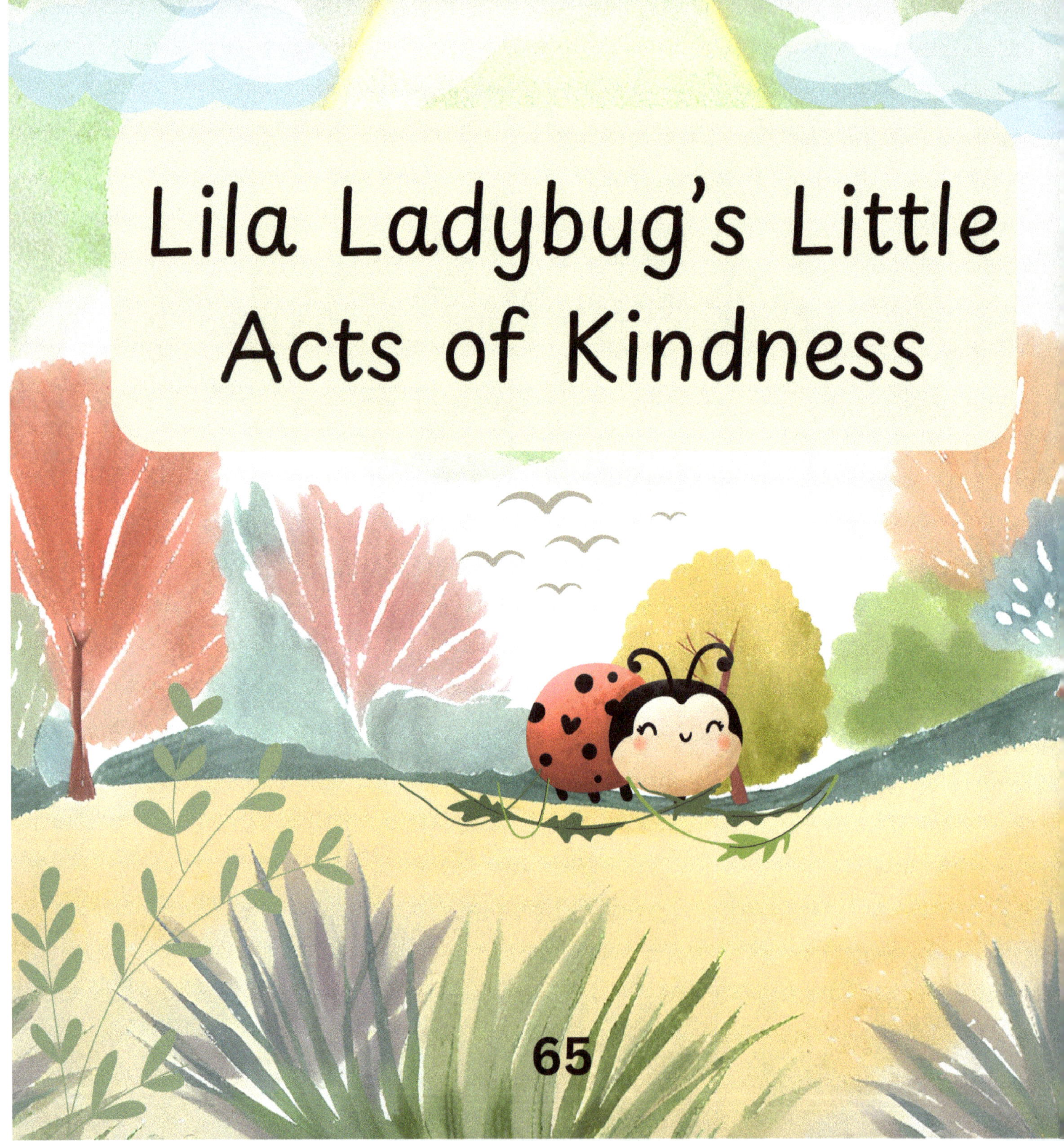

Lila Ladybug's Little
Acts of Kindness

Lila the Ladybug notices how some of her friends are feeling down.

She decides to do small acts of kindness,
like helping a snail find a new leaf.

Than she decides to sing a cheerful song
to a sad frog.

Her tiny gestures brighten everyone's day.

She inspires her friends to spread kindness too, making their little corner of the world happier.

Lila will try to help her friends more often.

71

Life Lesson: Small Actions Can Make a Big Difference

Sammy Squirrel's Save-the-Nuts Plan
73

Sammy Squirrel is excited about the coming winter but hasn't stored enough nuts.

As his friends prepare, he realizes he needs a plan.

He gathers his friends to discuss the best ways to collect and store nuts for the winter.
76

They create a fun schedule and work together.

By the end of the season, Sammy has enough nuts, and he learns the importance of planning ahead.

He understands that preparing for the future can lead to success and security.

Life Lesson: Planning for the
Future

The End